MW00636555

Judith Clancy

The Alluring World
of
Maiko and Geiko

Tankosha

Contents

Chapter *3*

The Seasons

The Alluring World of Maiko and Geiko

Copyright © 2016 by Judith Clancy
Photographs copyright © 2016 by Hiroshi Mizobuchi
Designed by Mio Onishi
Published by Tankosha Publishing Co., Ltd.,
Horikawa-dori Kuramaguchi-agaru, Kita-ku, Kyoto, Japan 603-8588
http://www.tankosha.co.jp

First edition January 2016   Second edition September 2016

All rights reserved. No part of this publication may be reproduced, stored in a
retrieval system, or transmitted in any form, or by any means, electronic, mechanical,
photocopying, recording or otherwise, without the prior permission of the publisher.

ISBN978-4-473-04059-6

Printed in Japan

Maiko and *Geiko* name cards

Introduction

Enticing, exotic, ephemeral—the words allude to an enthralling mystique: matt-white make up, tiny ruby-red lips, long sweeps of raven-black hair framing the face. Nowhere else but in Japan, and especially in Kyoto, the ancient capital, does this realm of beauty and womanhood exist—*Maiko* and *Geiko*.

It began centuries ago, on the sandy banks of the Kamo River where today, most of the *maiko* and *geiko* districts remain nearby with the exception of one in the northwest part of the city.

From 1200 years ago, after the capital was established, massive Buddhist temples were constructed for believers to pray for salvation. Shinto shrines, the preserve of the Emperor, performed court rituals to ensure the continuation of the Imperial line. The architecture of both religions represented some of the finest structures in Asia, huge buildings borrowing continental design, and gates constructed of native timber. As the city grew, Japanese culture began to establish itself as unique and different from neighboring China. Artisans and craftsmen perfected their skills making finer and finer goods to meet the needs of the court and residents. Sericulture reached Japan via the Korean peninsula in the 6th century and the art of dyeing and weaving produced robes similar to the form they are

today. Japan's interest in Chinese architecture, painting, ceramics, and calligraphy further helped redefine a native aesthetic standard. Kyoto developed into one of the world's most sophisticated cities by the 10th century.

Visitors entered the capital to petition the Shinto gods and Buddha, purchase charms to keep misfortune away, and learn how to better follow the dictates of Buddhist law. These masses also needed refreshment, so stalls and simple structures were set up to provide rest and repast. At first, it might have been a serving girl with a nice voice, saucy attitude, witty tongue, or gift for dance that brought a teahouse more customers. Over the centuries, new aesthetic standards emerged as musicians, playwrights, and actors were welcomed on all levels of society. By the 19th century, the capital represented the apex of Japanese artistic refinement and elegance. In its entertainment districts, beautiful wooden buildings (*ochaya*, literally, tea houses) established a construction standard intended strictly for entertainment purposes. Customers dined on exquisite cuisine presented on fine ceramics and lacquer ware, served by women elegantly clothed in dyed and embroidered silk robes.

With all the temples and shrines, Kyoto was, and still is, a religious center, but with a kind of spirituality that does not deny its believers the pleasures of the secular world. Japanese gods love song, dance, food and drink, and festivals honoring the deities tend to be

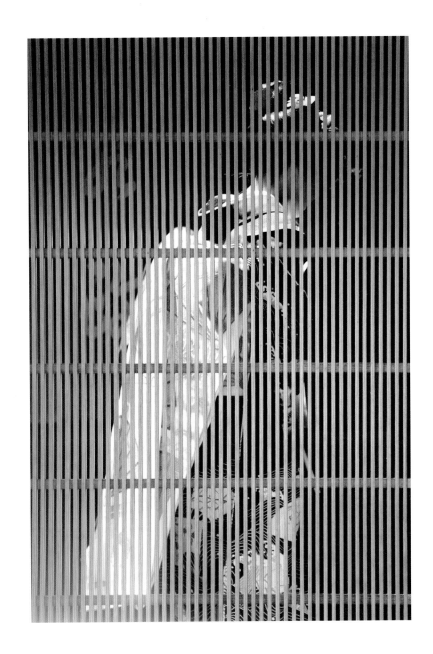

joyful, rousing affairs fueled by tiny cups of potent *sake*. By the early 18th century, several areas devoted to such earthly delights lined the back streets and narrow alleyways between the Kamo River and Gion-sha, now known as Yasaka Shrine.

Today, there are five areas known as *Gokagai*, literally Five Flower Districts, the famed pleasure quarters renown in Kabuki and Bunraku puppet plays and in painting and song—home to its professional entertainers. The *Kagai* continues to preserve Japanese traditional performing arts in a style befitting its reputation, and its cultural icons: *maiko* and *geiko*.

Willows line some of Kyoto's old streets, their supple branches redolent of fine dance movements, and their sturdy trunks resilient to passing storms, characteristics that embody *geiko*. Like the beauty of a bud about to open, until it reaches its flowering fulfillment, the women who entertain within the Flower Districts, are the codification of a culture that honors, respects, and understands transient beauty. A pleasing face is certainly an asset but the Japanese eye for beauty reaches far beyond the superficial to include posture, gait, language, deportment, and the ability to transform a gesture into a distinctive, memorable pose. Charm reveals itself in the lowered gaze of the young *maiko*, languid body movement, perfectly maintained coiffure, flawless skin, and a demure expression. Wrapped in layers of supple silk kimono, the body is completely obscured, with only the tantalizing nape of the neck hinting at the sensual being within.

Geiko, as Kyoto geisha are known, even while young, represent a more mature beauty although she may be only a few years older than the apprentice *maiko*. Years of experience clearly reveal a greater refinement, more polished performing skills, and a personal repartee that have gained her fans and admirers. As a hostess and entertainer, she is in demand for special occasions and events while also being in charge of overseeing the cultural education of her apprentice *maiko*. Her chief responsibility is to make a social occasion proceed as smoothly as possible to every guest's satisfaction while not dominating the gathering. Her professional skills as a hostess call on her to flatter, cajole, and appease with a near invisible influence

The process of turning a young woman into an apprentice *maiko* begins when she has completed junior high school, the end of compulsory education in Japan. At sixteen, young women can apply to be accepted into one of the Flower Districts by a letter of introduction and more recently online. Once her application is accepted, she travels to Kyoto for a formal interview. Long ago, many of the daughters born to *geiko* remained in the districts, brought up to assume their mothers' work. In 2015, there were only six Kyotoites among the sixty-five *maiko*, most of them born far outside the region. Almost half have traveled hundreds of kilometers to fulfill their dreams of training to reach their goal as *maiko*, and eventually the exalted status of *geiko*.

Lessons in song and dance are among the most rigorous lessons, so it helps if the young woman has already studied dance and a traditional instrument, in addition to showing a natural ability to perform on stage and having agreeable social skills.

Her life begins under the instruction of her new "mother," (*okaa-san*) in an *okiya*, a place where these women live together with their "older sisters" (*onee-san*) who they can observe, and learn the proper greetings and manners expected of them as residents of the district.

Learning Kyoto's distinct dialect is a first step followed by the language peculiar to the Flower World. New words, expressions, and intonation must be adopted while they learn to temper their voices as well as their gait. Gone are ordinary shoes. From now on, feet covered with cloven cloth *tabi* socks slip into the traditional footwear, elegant *zori* or wooden summer *geta*. Lessons are attended in silk kimono or cotton summer *yukata*, layers of clothing that affect one's posture and bearing, and slow one's stride.

The beginner lets her hair grow long so it can be fashioned into the elaborate coiffure worn by *maiko*. Cushions of false hair are woven into the crown to secure the natural tresses and hold in place additional hair ornaments.

Unless one has been brought up in a traditional household, these external changes are the easiest to get accustomed to. The coming two or three years of disciplined life of daily lessons before reaching the rank of *maiko* are much more difficult and will transform their lives forever.

Besides the role as professional entertainer and hostess, the *maiko* and *geiko* of the Flower Districts are the purveyors of traditional rites and practices that season the Japanese calendar. Asking the guidance of their teachers for the new year, scattering good-luck beans in early February, performing tea ceremonies under blooming plum trees later in the month, participating in a major festivals to presenting gifts to their elders in appreciation for all the help received during the year are elaborate events unto themselves, and featured on local and national TV. Their presence assures a tacit promise to the cultural heart of Japan to keep these practices relevant and alive.

Chapter 1

The People

People of the *Kagai*

The women of the *geiko/maiko kagai* districts are bound—and not just by the snugly wound *obi* sash that secures their kimono. They also are constrained by the tight customs and tacit rules of the "flower-and-willow world" to which they are committed and by the lifestyle they strive to preserve. (The reference comes from equating the district's women with the uncontested beauty of flowers and the ability of willows to bend in a storm and retain their graceful pose.)

That is not to say that their world is unchanging. It has evolved greatly since the last century, and most markedly in the last decade. No longer is it a place, as it was for centuries before, where impoverished families sent girls to become indentured servants assured of three meals a day and with the possibility of ascending to the rank and comfortable life of the talented *geiko*.

Today, with the advent of the Internet, young teenagers from all over the country can apply online, come to Kyoto, and if accepted, pursue the dream of a glamorous life and an appreciative audience. Novels, movies, and TV have shaped those dreams, and generated a strong, romanticized appeal. But what has remained constant in this male-dominated country is that the flower world is prominently a female realm—albeit one determined by male standards of grace and beauty. Men play a part in the life of *geiko* and *maiko*, but mainly as respected teachers, talented chefs, dressers and, of course, valued customers.

In the past, a young girl entered the *kagai* district on the sixth day of the sixth month at the age of six. In today's Japan, where high school is not compulsory, girls can apply during junior high school, and enter the *kagai* from age sixteen. They come to Kyoto with their parents for an interview and to meet their prospective associates. If accepted, these novices (*shikomi*, from the verb to teach and train) begin their induction. The first step involves intensive training in the Kyoto dialect, a soft, formal pattern of speech, unlike the clipped cadence of northern tongues. They also study proper greetings and terms of address for each rank of person whom they will encounter, the intricacies of Kyoto-style *kaiseki* cuisine, local customs, and religious practices. But perhaps most importantly, the novices learn to unquestioningly obey their elders.

During the very strict first year, they have little time to contact their families, as they make the transition from their birth mother to their new "mother" (*okaa-san*), the proprietress of the *okiya*, where they and others reside.

Another *okiya* resident, just one or two years older, will become their new "older sister" (*onee-san*). The new recruit will learn to behave by imitating her, reinforcing the bond between them while absorbing the tacit rules that bind the residents of the *okiya* together.

Today, the allure of the city of Kyoto and its distinct culture draw most applicants from the countryside, where farming, fishing and forestry, and related industries dominate occupational options. Consequently, only six of Kyoto's *geiko* and *maiko* are from Kyoto; the other sixty hail from regions outside the city.

The stories behind the novice's dreams and motives are as diverse as the young women themselves, but they are united most often by their artistry.

The *okaa-san* puts the final touch on a *maiko* before leaving the *ochaya* teahouse.

Shikomi
—teenage trainee—

Long ago, the sixth day of the sixth month in the sixth year of a girl's life was the day designated for her to enter an *okiya*. In this house, she would learn the arts of becoming a member of the flower-and-willow world, the *kagai*. Although the daughter of a *geiko* may still enter an *okiya*, today, most of the applicants come from outside this world. Many from far distant prefectures can now apply online and await an invitation to travel to Kyoto to be interviewed.

If chosen and perseverant, they will undergo a Pygmalian transformation and become worldly, skilled in performing arts, elegantly attired in kimono, and graceful—the stuff of teenage dreams, an object of desire—a codified display of culture and tradition. Books, movies, and TV offer glimpses into the intriguing lives of the *maiko* of Kyoto, and can ignite irresistible curiosity.

The proprietress of the *okiya* may then invite the young woman (usually sixteen years of age) and her parents to Kyoto. There, she will be interviewed and spend a few days learning about a trainee's obligations and duties, and meet some of her contemporaries and superiors.

After returning home, if her parents consent, the family will return to Kyoto to sign a non-binding contract with the *okiya*. The young woman will then bid farewell to her parents and begin training.

For the first year, she will address the proprietress of the *okiya* as *okaa-san* (mother) and the older *maiko* as *onee-san* (older sister). An older sister will guide her through the daily routines, introduce the dance teachers; and together with her new mother, instill a ready obedience and an ability to respond to any request cheerfully and quickly. For an intense year, the apprentice must learn all this as well as how to convey the special image of the *kagai* she will represent. The *okiya* is a world unto itself where the teenager must absorb the fine social skills needed to entertain in a *zashiki* or performing a tea ceremony. Increasingly, overwhelmed teenagers reconsider their choice of lifestyle, and a majority return to their hometowns.

The *shikomi* novice accompanies *maiko* on their way to appointments as part of her training.

Voice of the
~Shikomi~

Straight-backed and as attentive as possible, two fresh-faced and wide-eyed sixteen-year-olds watched the older women of the kagai glide through the office foyer on their ways to and from lessons. Both trainees were wearing jeans and hooded sweatshirts, and despite the casual clothing, they were recognized as newcomers and their anxiously correct greetings returned with courtesy. Sunlight glistened on their shoulder-length raven-black hair as they eagerly responded to questions about their new lives.

One teenager, after a quick, shy glance at her co-trainee, said she had dreamed of becoming a *maiko* since kindergarten and began dance lessons while very young. Although she was an only child, her parents agreed to her decision to leave home. Her love of dancing and the allure of tales of old Japan, especially those of famous *maiko*, helped her decide to forego high school and continue dancing.

The other teenager, slightly chagrined, admitted to not having any special talent, but was greatly attracted to the culture of the ancient capital after meeting a *maiko* who was on tour. *Maiko* are the iconic face of Kyoto on most travel posters and appear at promotional events. The refined image of the visitor stayed with the rural teenager, helping her decide to undergo a year of the strict training necessary to mold her into a similarly graceful, traditional woman. She left behind an older brother and sister, and although very busy, misses them—and her mother's cooking.

Both the giggly teenagers concur that one of the hardest things to master is sitting Japanese-style for long periods and sleeping in hard futons on *tatami*. In traditional Japan, much of life was lived on the straw floor-matted *tatami* floor, without chairs and sitting at low tables when dining. While men sat cross-legged, except in formal situations, women were required always to sit on their knees, legs tucked decorously under them. Nowadays, most homes have kitchen tables, chairs, and beds, so the reversion to tradition can be literally painful for the young recruits. An added discomfort is the *okiya's* well balanced diet with its absence of junk food and snacks, and the lack of TV and Internet.

Daily vigilance—following orders, doing things exactly as demanded, maintaining perfect posture, speaking only when spoken to—is as strict now as it was long ago. Not surprisingly, roughly just a third of the novices decide to continue after the first year away from home. The dreamers are shifted out, and only those with great determination endure and pass the initial trial. Once the young trainee reaches the rank of *maiko*, however, she is more likely to remain.

Shikomi novices who have begun training the same year.

Maiko

After completing a year as a novice in the *kagai* district, a teenager begins to learn in earnest how to become a *maiko*. Until now, she has worn regular clothes, even jeans, since many of her duties involve running errands and helping her older "sister" prepare for an evening's performance at an *ochaya* restaurant where the *zashiki* entertainment is held.

Nowadays, most young women have very little experience wearing kimono and traditional footwear. The posture and gait these require are transformative, and it takes more than a little practice to appear graceful and at ease. During the one- or two-year training period, the girls' hair grows long enough to wear up, a requirement for fashioning the five or so traditional hairstyles that allow the addition of hair ornaments to complement a kimono's seasonal motifs and to accent the formality of the occasion. Dating from the 18th century, these hairstyles are still considered the mark of a refined woman, but are a challenge to maintain. A hard wooden block serves as a nighttime neck pillow designed to keep the head and hairdo several inches off the floor.

Walking gracefully on uneven, stone-inlaid streets or climbing stairs in high wooden clogs is another feat to be mastered. Toppling over is unthinkable, but several women confessed to coming close to that embarrassing experience.

The older sister, *onee-san*, and mother, *okaa-san*, teach the novice skills such as applying make-up. The characteristic white powdered face is a throwback to a time when dark interiors, lit only with oil lamps, made it difficult to see the entertainer's features. The face is prepared with a light coat of camellia oil that helps the dusting of white powder, mixed with water and applied with a brush, adhere to the skin. A special metal fork-like form is rested against the back of the neck, and around that, the neck is painted white, leaving all but two stripes of skin unpowdered. This pattern enhances focus on the nape of the neck as a beauty point, and offers a subtle erotic hint of the bare skin beneath. A touch of red on the bottom lip indicates the *maiko* is in her first year of training. Thereafter, both upper and lower lips will be reddened.

On becoming a *maiko*, the women are expected to be proficient in calligraphy, tea ceremony, and *Ikebana* flower arrangement. But the hardest part of a *maiko*'s training is the dance lessons. The teachers are strict, even severe according to some, and becoming accomplished requires hours and hours of practice. The aspirant must pass a final test in front of her teachers, elders, and peers before she is recognized as ready to embark as a professional *maiko* and gain an audience's approval.

Formally dressed in a long-sleeved kimono, elaborate hair ornaments, *darari-obi* sash and high *okobo* clogs.

Voice of the
~ Maiko ~

A fission of tension rippled through the two maiko as they waited to appear on stage. Apparent, too, as they responded to questions, was their keen awareness that their replies would reflect on the reputation of their residence. Their silver hair ornaments sparkled under the backstage lighting as they nodded in response, perfectly groomed in extravagantly colorful kimono. Their identical facial make-up—matt-white, highlighted in touches of red—somehow illuminated their individual beauty.

Both *maiko* came from rural areas, were circumspect, unfailingly polite, and very guarded. Their demeanor, after two years of training, revealed mastery of what was expected of them.

Asked how they started down this path, one mentioned that she had become interested in the *maiko's* life through a book. Another told of an older sister's excited tale of meeting a *maiko* who had come to dance in the prefecture where they lived.

Mastering the Kyoto dialect was one of the first difficulties as, of course, was doing well in dance lessons under the renown fifth-generation head of the Inoue School of *Kyomai*, Yachiyo Inoue. Inoue's reputation and strict teaching methods are known throughout Japan, and the school she heads is highly regarded among performers of classical dance. Both these young novices strive to be worthy of the school's reputation.

Another difficulty is maintaining their elaborate hairstyles between weekly hairdresser appointments. Somewhat thankfully, their very busy schedule of lessons every morning and dance performances at nightly *zashiki* appointments leave them exhausted enough to manage sleep on the fifteen-centimeter-high wooden block pillows that protect their hairdos. Six days a week, they return late at night to a shared room, and rise at about eight in the morning. This hectic schedule provides little chance to reflect on their lives, much less on their future beyond the immediate goal: ascending to the rank of *geiko*.

Besides learning to perform the tea ceremony, and write beautiful calligraphy, they must maintain the expected level of polite greetings and responses—no matter how trival the task. Their reputations, and those of the *okiya* where they reside, depend on it.

Nowadays, because of all the time and money invested in the women, they are asked to sign a five-year, non-binding contract on entering the *kagai* at sixteen years of age. They can leave at any time, but quitting is less of a stigma after fulfilling the contract and at least partially satisfying all those who have invested their time and effort in teaching them.

Asked how they deal with the many tourists who surround them to ask for a photo when they travel to their appointments, they quietly said that they just maintain a calm expression, eyes straight ahead, and keep moving. This passive forbearance reveals much of how they cope with the attention that comes with their chosen lives.

Dance lessons in Miyagawa-cho.

Maiko Hairstyles

1. *Wareshinobu*

2. *Ofuku*

3. *Yakko-shimada*

4. *Katsuyama*

5. *Sakkou*

1. The first year
2. The second year
3. Formal occasions
4. During the Gion Festival
5. During her last week as Maiko

Hana-kanzashi
—*Maiko* hair ornaments through the year—

January

Auspicious combination
of pine, bamboo, plum

February

Plum blossoms

March

Canola blossoms

April

Cherry blossoms

May

Wisteria

June

Willow with fringed pinks

July

Round fans

August

Pampas grass

September

Bellflowers

October

Chrysanthemums

November

Maples

December

Kabuki *Maneki* signboards

Each month is represented with stylized hair ornaments.

Applying matt-white make-up

Two lines on ordinary occasions.

Three lines on formal occasions.

When making her debut, only the bottom lip is painted scarlet.

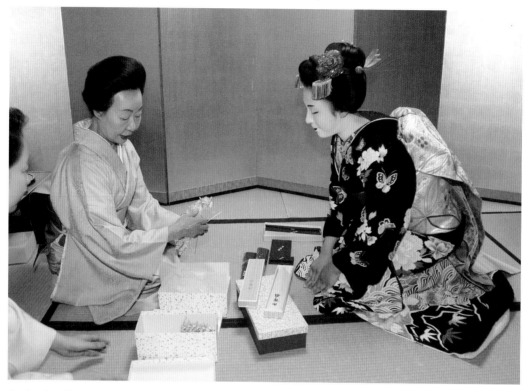

On the day of her debut, the *okaa-san* presents the *maiko* with a small gift.

The bond between the *maiko* (left) and her *onee-san* older sister is as strong as a family tie. The older sister has the responsibility to teach and guide the younger woman as she navigates the unspoken rules of the *kagai*.

Geiko

By about age twenty, a *maiko* has the opportunity to officially declare her intention to remain in the *kagai* and become a *geiko*.

If she wishes to continue, she will be tested and assessed by her peers, teachers, and all her associates. She will be expected to reflect the standards of deportment, talent, and graciousness of the district she represents, and with her teachers' and peers' approval, she will be elevated to the status of *geiko*.

If she declines to take this step, she is free to leave the *kagai* to return home to consider her future, be it more education or a service-related job.

Once the choice is made, she will continue to dance, but will also learn to sing and to play an instrument. As her popularity grows, her presence will be requested, ensuring her of a steady income in this world of playful innuendo and tete-a-tete that is a part of an evening's entertainment. The long, busy days required mean she often won't return to her *okiya* residence until midnight. With almost every hour accounted for, a *geiko*'s life lacks the leisure one might envision. But by skillfully fulfilling her duties to entertain, she can build a clientele who will request her services in the future.

The ceremony that marks her becoming a *geiko* is called *Erikae*—literally, changing the collar. Not only will the collar of her kimono be worn at a less revealing angle, her hairstyle will become less elaborate, and her kimono will be more understated in color and pattern. Her *obi* will no longer hang free, but be rounded in back, in *taiko-obi* (drum-shaped) style popularly worn by many music and tea teachers as well as by ordinary women outside the pleasure quarters of the *kagai*.

Her duties, too, will evolve. As a *geiko*, she is expected to have the experience and skill to ensure that an evening's entertainment progresses smoothly, and that everyone is content and satisfied by the dancing, singing, banquet, and atmosphere. Her conversation should be as charming as it is witty to encourage even the more retiring guests to participate in an enjoyable manner.

Her income will still come from the *okiya*, depending on the number of *zashiki* parties she attends at the official *ochaya* restaurants, as well as private parties at which her presence is requested. Increasingly, the tourist industry now arranges lunches and dinners where a *geiko* or *maiko* dance for, and afterward, chat with guests.

She will no longer rely on her sponsoring house, *okiya*, to provide clothing, but must start to assemble her own wardrobe with money from her work. Earnings from major dance recitals,

Holding up her kimono, the *geiko* reveals the gorgeous silk undergarment.

On becoming a *geiko*, the hairstyle and kimono reflect a mature elegance.

however, including biannual dance revenues, are a reliable source of income, with the *Ookini Zaidan* organization managing advertising and ticket sales. Money paid by *ochaya* guests who attend *zashiki* is pooled and redistributed to each house by the *Ochaya* Association.

During this time, a *geiko* may deepen ties to her customers and fans, making lifelong friends of some, and occasionally, marrying if she so chooses. At times, *geiko* and *maiko* may be asked out to dinner by a customer, but certain rules apply. *Ochaya* guests have been introduced by existing customers, with the understanding that they are expected to act with discretion in their dealings with *ochaya* personnel and *geiko* and *maiko*. To act improperly, would embarrass the recommending associate, and result in the guest's being barred from the *ochaya*.

A man requesting a dinner date must telephone the proprietress of the *ochaya* or *okiya*. Being seen with a *geiko* or *maiko* is considered as quite a boon for a young man—somewhat akin to having a glamorous movie star on one's arm. For a *maiko*, this formal date is about the limit of her allowed interaction with the opposite sex. Absorbed in the world of lessons, isolated from family, old friends, and media, *maiko* live in a very different world from their contemporaries. As to be expected, their conversational skills revolve around daily routine and a little harmless *okiya* gossip.

Never do *geiko* or *maiko* discuss what has happened in the *ochaya* or during a *zashiki*. To do so would be anathema to the profession and possibly to others, as one *geiko* learned when her indiscretion ended the career of a politician.

A dinner invitation for a *geiko*, even if she lives apart from the *kagai*, also comes via her former *okaa-san*. After the formal request, though, the option of extending the evening beyond the meal is entirely up to the woman. That the *ochaya* proprietress has vetted this customer and given permission for them to meet, means that the gentleman is of good reputation and will remain as discrete as she. The relationship may be short term, but can turn into a lasting friendship as well. Occasionally, a couple may decide to marry, and the occasion will be marked by a simple ceremony ending her career as a *geiko*.

Geiko can also retire if they wish, and some do, going on to careers in restaurant or bar management, galleries, or as art consultants. Her past association with actors, artists and restaurateurs assures her of a variety of opportunities.

A *geiko* sings as she strums the *shamisen* while a *maiko* plays the "Konpira-fune-fune" game.

29

Voice of the
~Geiko~

It was a warm humid day, but the geiko, appeared in a light, summer kimono and simple obi as fresh as clear sparkling water, glided into the room. Not a wisp of hair was out of place despite the humidity. Without even a dab of make-up, her unblemished complexion and lively dark eyes revealed a classic beauty. Her bearing was exquisite, even majestic for someone in her thirties.

The *geiko* had become interested in the *kagai* after her father was transferred to Kyoto. The family lived nearby and knew the neighborhood and its residents. While in junior high, she often saw *maiko* and *geiko* on a daily basis. Their elaborate kimono coupled with wholesomeness charmed her. Her parents gave permission, and she signed the required non-binding contract with the proprietress of a prominent *okiya*.

Like many *geiko*, the thirty-year-old confesses to not always taking care of her health, in part because she has little time to grocery shop. Her days and nights are regularly filled with lessons, learning new dances and songs, and arranging her wardrobe for the evening's appointments. She lives in a district known for its weaving and dyeing, so her artful choice of clothing is especially telling to knowledgeable guests. The kind of fine woven and dyed kimono and *obi* she is expected to wear can cost thousands of dollars, and are an important reflection of her taste and status.

She lives in an apartment near the *kagai*, pays rent, and buys her own kimono with income from performing at *zashiki* or from entertaining at private parties. During the summer, she is present at a beer garden in her district that features the presence of *geiko* and *maiko*. They may be asked to sing or perform an impromptu dance for which they may receive a little gratuity.

Today, these women are professional entertainers. They contribute to pension funds, as well as paying national, municipal, and city taxes. Freed from the pre-war possibility of poverty in old age or dependency on children they might have, many prefer to continue their life of performing.

Another geiko apologized for being slightly behind schedule, while never betraying the imposition the meeting must have caused her. Her upswept hair was elegantly styled, framing a creamy complexion, a little flushed from haste, but smooth as a young girl's. The only hint of age came from the subdued color of her dyed silk kimono, a misty shade of lavender. She laughed easily when asked about her past fifty years in the kagai, delighted at the chance to recall some of her older, witty customers and near-embarrassing moments when she walked home a bit too tipsy in the early morning light.

This *geiko* came from a big family in Fushimi, a ward in southern Kyoto. Her year-older sister, perhaps lonely for family, had urged her to join the *kagai* pleasure quarters where she was a *maiko*. While acting as a kind of waitress, the younger sister learned to greet customers, serve food in the proper order using utensils and dishware appropriate to the season, and run errands for the head of the *ochaya* restaurant.

She was able to attend the nearby high school during the day, but rushed back to help prepare for the night's events. Her older sister, after three years as a *maiko*, quit at the age of nineteen to marry, and now lives in Tokyo near her children and grandchildren.

The younger sister, accustomed to her life in the *kagai*, decided to remain and went on to become a *maiko* and then a *geiko*.

She had played the stringed *shamisen* for decades until a recent bout of carpal tunnel syndrome forced her to retire that instrument. But at the age of sixty-four, she still stars in the annual dance revues, occasionally sings, and plays the small shoulder drum.

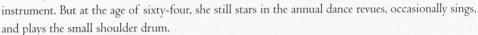

She lives independent from, but close to, the *kagai* district where she works. She laments her lack of culinary skills and time to prepare healthy meals, and often relies on the local noodle shop for a quick meal before going to an appointment. (Since neither *geiko* nor *maiko* sit and eat with the guests, they have to make an effort to eat balanced meals.)

Her face lit with smiles as she recounted when a wealthy customer suddenly declared that everyone must travel to a hot spring on the Japan Sea coast during the winter months to enjoy a banquet of crab. Instruments and appropriate kimono were packed, train tickets would appear, and a party of ten or more would set off for an overnight's fun of singing, dancing, and of course exquisite cuisine.

She now counts her customers and their families as friends, even as extended family at times. Her past and future work as a performer brings her a sense of accomplishment and pride.

In the shadow of the flower world

The old system under which women, confined to licensed pleasure quarters, found patrons who supported—and expected an intimate relationship in return—is no long a feasible or a viable means of support. In the 17th cetury, Japan was rife with prostitution, and to control and contain, and perhaps profit from this trade, the government created an enclosed pleasure district a little outside of the city of *Edo* (now Tokyo). By the 19th century, the area and others, in Osaka, and in Kyoto, housed thousands of young women from extremely poor families who led wretched lives as indentured servants. The woman's only chance of escaping this life was if a wealthy customer desired her, bought her contract, and took her as a second wife. This system of brothels existed until after World War II when prostitution became illegal in 1958.

The *geiko* of Kyoto however, were never considered prostitutes, but professional entertainers, which they ultimately are. Unfortunately, even today, the word *geisha* is connected with prostitution, the mention of which bridles the *geiko* of Kyoto.

Gion Kobu maiko circa 1937.

Dance, drum, and transverse flute lessons in Miyagawa-cho.

Jikata

While beauty and youth are prized, talent is also highly valued in the *kagai*. The *jikata*, many of whom are older and have gained great skill, provide musical accompaniment during an evening's entertainment at an *ochaya* or during one of the major dance revues held in the spring and fall.

The teachers of *jikata* are mostly men, many from Kabuki or Noh, who pass along the strict methods required to master the ancient instruments used in these theatrical traditions.

All the women had started off as dancers and must master that art, some favor singing or playing a traditional instrument such as the *shamisen* (a three-stringed instrument with a long neck, played with an ivory plectrum or plucked by fingers for a softer effect) or *kotsutsumi* (a small hand-drum that rests on the shoulder). Others play a small *taiko* floor drum that is struck with sticks; *yokubue* (a transverse flute), or *teuchi* (hand clapping as an accompaniment).

Although one's skill often rises with age and experience, so too, can physical limitations. The hours of practice on an instrument needed to achieve the tension to convey a change of pace or phrasing require strong wrists, and inflammation is a risk. One woman also lamented that diminishing hearing made it difficult to properly tune an instrument or hear cues.

Some *geiko* are known for singing *kouta* and *nagauta*, traditional ballads and songs rich in poetic reference to the seasons, and love songs of a bawdy or subtly erotic nature.

It takes a learned listener to catch the cultural references and cross-references, and a skilled performer to master the necessarily large and ready repertoire.

Jikata musicians sing and play the drums, flute and *shamisen* at the Ponto-cho dance revue.

Voice of the
~Jikata~

The former geiko's voice commanded attention, and her eyes radiated merriment as she shared some of her eighty-years of life in the kagai. A reminder of years of fine meals, her generous girth was contained by a warm grey obi. The color of her kimoono was appropriate to her age, and she had commissioned playful motifs to be dyed onto it, revealing a jovial spirit that many younger women might envy.

She had entered the world officially at the age of six on the sixth day of the sixth month as was custom long ago. Now in her eighties, the musical accompanist was born to a *geiko* in Gion Kobu and expected to follow her mother. When still a small child, she was frightend by the strictness of the dance doyen, Yachiyo Inoue, and froze at the thought of dance lessons. Through her mother's introduction, she entered an *okiya* in the Ponto-cho district and began her training there. She started to learn *tokiwazu* singing from the age of ten, as well as *shamisen*. She became a *geiko* at twenty after being tested in front of her teachers and peers, an occasion she still recalls with pride.

She reminisced how greatly the *kagai* has changed. In the 1980s, Japan had emerged from the devastation of World War II. Salaried men, under great pressure to succeed, wanted a chance to let off steam. The *kagai* were filled with company workers eager to be entertained, to party, sing and totally relax in a reliable environment. The shops along Nishiki-koji bustled with businesses supplying the places of entertainment with culinary delicacies. Those days are mostly behind, she said, but there are still a good number of influential customers who come. However, more and more, the trade caters to events that include tourists. Dancing and games entertain the guests, and appearance seems more important than in the old days when it was imperarive to master one's lessons and to give attention to individual customers rather than to groups. Nowadays, she said, many of the events involve customers taking photos with the *geiko* and *maiko* before the entertainment begins.

On a personal level, client satisfaction gave her a great sense of accomplishment, and she felt her skill and charm could make any evening successful. She laughed jovially as she recalled being feted and dined, and blushed to remember how she sometimes ordered the most expensive item on the menu rather than the cheapest as she should have done. Ah, youth.

At eighty-five, she is still taking lessons on the *shamisen*, and chuckles with amusement that now most teachers are younger than she. She doesn't expect to retire and still receives a salary from performing. One of the biggest problems for older musicians like her is hearing loss that limits the ability to properly tune the *shamisen*. Another difficulty is painful knees from sitting on the floor for hours. Most of her repertoire is memorized, but with age, she feels more confident when she has the score in front of her and a small seat under her.

Miyako-no-Nigiwai.

Music within the *Kagai* district

Japan has a long and rich history of songs, ballads, recited poetry, and instrumental music. Music is an essential skill for the *maiko* and *geiko*, be it mastery of song and dance or an assured competence on an instrument.

Written records of *Kouta*, short narrative songs, date back to the 14th century. By the 16th century, the *sanshin*, a precursor of the *shamisen*, was introduced. Another type of song, *nagauta*, involves more storytelling than poetic sentiment, but often the richness of the medium lies in the singer's voice and her ability to express the emotional content and versatility of the *shamisen*.

Songs of love and parting are popular, as well as more titillating tunes. Sentimentality has an honored place in Japanese music, which often tugs the heartstrings with memories of one-sided love, a nostalgic countryside, or regrets of moments missed. The nasal, high-pitched vocalization

flavors the theme and setting, and the tense, even jarring, use of the plectrum embellishes the story line and emotional content.

The genre requires listeners who are learned enough to recognize cultural references in the lyrics. Mention of a small, four-and-a-half *tatami*-sized room, for example, suggests an encounter, the details of which may be left to the listener's imagination. This is the standard-sized room for the tea ceremony, and the reference can convey a tender sentiment passing between two guests as they partake of the brew, or it might indicate a couple meeting for an intimate tryst.

The vocalization may sound strident to unaccustomed ears, but the lyrics engage the listener in moving and even humorous ways, depending on the performer. A talented *jikata* with a large and evocative vocal range is much sought after.

Vocal and instrumental score.

A lesson in singing a *tokiwazu* ballad with a *shamisen* accompaniment.

The strings of the *shamisen* are plucked by a plectrum.

The small *kotsutsumi* hand drum rests on the shoulder while being struck by the hand.

Okiya Proprietress (okaa-san)

The *okiya* serves as a residence for the young *shikomi* trainees, *maiko* and even some *geiko* if they wish to continue to live there. The rooms are spare, and initially several teenagers may share quarters. Here, the young trainee meets her new mother and older sister who will guide her through the rigors of dance lessons, the protocol of Kyoto customs, social rank, proper greetings, duties, and obligations within the *kagai* district.

The proprietress will arrange all the meals, make sure the room and all its contents remain in order, teach the trainee how to put on and wear a kimono with all its seasonal requirements, and introduce her to the people related to her studies. She also handles finances, sees that the women are cared for when ill, and gives them the support to reach their goals.

The young women are taught to be unfailingly polite, never talk back to or make demands on any of their seniors (quite a task for recent junior high school graduates away from home), and remain dedicated to their studies. The *okiya* owner must bond with her young charge, as with any adopted child, and foster good relations with the other older women in her care. The reputation of the house depends on her good and steady judgment, so each of her charges must always reflect the proprietress' guiding philosophy and discipline.

A nallow street in Miyagawa-cho.

Geiko and *maiko* give their New Year greetings to *okaa-san*.

Voice of the
~ Okiya Proprietress ~

The proprietress led the way with a slow, deliberate grace bespeaking her position after eighty-years of life within the kagai. Her kimono, in understated floral designs on a rich shade of grey, was a product of some of the best kimono artisans in Kyoto. With the slightest movement of her well-groomed hand, cups of fragrant tea appeared before us. She spoke with an assurance that only a woman whose life had spanned so many decades of experience could.

An only child, the proprietress succeeded her mother and grandmother as head of the *okiya*. Now she cannot imagine doing any other work, adding that she would do it all over again. She seems supremely comfortable in this world ruled by women, and looks to the future.

The pleasure quarters have lasted through wars, economic downturns, and an aging population, she says. That world, she acknowledges, was tinged by a history of impropriety, and even though it will never become an Intangible World Heritage, the *kagai* will continue to exist as long as Japanese culture persists.

The biggest challenge she foresees is the decline in performers' knowledge of traditional music and dance along with the increasing inability of audiences to appreciate the skill and references. She recognizes the easy popularity of karaoke among younger customers and is shrewd enough to accommodate such new styles of entertaining guests. Her district's beer garden is very popular with all ages. A great many of the regular customers are artisans from the nearby weaving and dyeing area, so they maintain a special interest in design, color, and new trends, and are attentive to what is being worn.

With proximity of one of Kyoto's largest shrines and its annual public tea ceremony, she has a special relationship with the world of tea. The districts are always in need of support, and when major repairs were called for about five years ago, a patron of the arts pledged financial help that allowed many of the *ochaya* to renovate. The rejuvenation of the Kamishichiken district, for example, inspired new shops and restaurants to open alongside the existing, well-known *ochaya*, making the area a must-see for many tourists who visit the nearby shrine. This accomplished, she is proud of her district and its assured place in the future of Kyoto.

Animated, yet reserved, the proprietress was dressed casually in slacks and a knit top—clothing that belied her status in this domain. Her ready smile revealed the warmth she feels for the women in her care. While talking about her past, she often paused to acknowledge contemporaries as they passed with a nod and a few words of greeting.

Born in Osaka to a family of four children, the woman's older sister entered a *kagai* in Kyoto. Although already married with a daughter, when her sister died suddenly, she was urged to move to Kyoto and take over that position. Acknowledging the help of many local residents, some of whom were passing by as we talked, she was able to learn to manage an *okiya* residence. She now feels very close to her young charges and grateful for the career thrust on her. Her daughter will take over her position when she retires.

A new crop of novices is essential to preserving this world. When interviewing aspiring young women during their initial stay of a few days, proprietors observe their behavior and earnestness. Personal motivation is extremely important.

There presently are nine young women under this women's supervision, learning proper language and dress. They share a room and have few personal belongings. (Most of the kimono and accessories they will wear belong to the *okiya*, some items having been cherished for decades.) The proprietress also emphasizes that she wants the young women to not only be good *maiko*, but cultivated people with good hearts as well. Physical requirements are few but being 160 centimeters in height and looking svelte in a kimono are considerations. The training is hard, and she lamented that nowadays, most young women decide to return to their hometowns.

When asked about the future of the *kagai*, she hopes people will remember this culture, the need for proper greetings, appropriate behavior in front of teachers, guests, and others, while recognizing that it would be difficult for it to be designated an Intangible World Heritage, as Kabuki and Noh drama have, because of its association with epicurean pleasures.

Aware that the economy is forcing change, she is trying to make an occasion with *maiko* entertainment more accessible to the general public. While most regular customers are still from Kyoto and Osaka, increasingly, the hospitality industry is having an impact, bringing in overseas and local tourists.

Otokoshi
—kimono dresser—

Within Gion Kobu, it is men who practice the art of dressing *geiko* and *maiko*. These *otokoshi* make certain that the women they serve are visions of grace and beauty who uphold the expectations of the district.

The dresser ensures that the elaborate layers of clothing that envelop a *maiko* are secured perfectly, lest she becomes disheveled. He watches that every woman who slips into her delicate footwear be perfectly adorned in silk robes. For the woman to go through the elaborate process takes up to an hour of putting on make-up, being dressed, and inserting the appropriate hair ornaments to accentuate their clothing, as well as dozens more tradition-dictated and creative details.

The first layer of underclothing is the *hada-juban*, a thin, long kimono-shaped garment of fine cotton secured only with long ties. This might be the most crucial step in the dresser's process. If the ties are even 1 or 2 millimeters off-center, the next layer of clothing will not be properly aligned.

The angle of the collar is another concern. A woman's neck is considered her most sensuous feature, and the proper angle of the collar highlights a smooth, sloping powdered neck. Good judgment is a prerequisite in determining how to best accentuate the woman's particular silhouette.

Next, a colorful silk under-robe is tied into place, topped by the kimono itself. Lastly, for the *maiko*, the dresser wraps a long brocade *obi* (sash), often weighing up to 5 kilos (11 lbs.), and ties it into the unique *darari*-style, characterized by two long lengths of brocade hanging free in back.

Geiko also are assisted when dressing, but their *taiko*-style obi is simpler, being tucked in and rounded, rather than trailing loose.

The *okiya* proprietress chooses hair ornaments and kimono.

The Gion Kobu district ranks highest among Kyoto's *ochaya*, with the greatest number of women and a stellar reputation for sophisticated *geiko* and *maiko* proficient in a style of dance taught by Yachiyo Inoue. But when it comes to the ensemble in which they appear, it is the dresser is who is responsible for perfection.

Two dressers ready a *maiko* for a formal appointment. Tying the brocade *obi* sash requires strength and precision.

The *maiko*'s extravagant lengths of brocade silk *obi* hang free (left).
The *geiko*'s obi sash is tucked and rounded in *taiko*-style (right).

Voice of the
~*Otokoshi*~

The two dressers in Gion Kobu appear robust and lithe as they lean back in the swivel chairs, delighted to talk about their work. One with an impish grin is clad in jeans and a bomber jacket. The other wears casual slacks and t-shirt. Their faces crease with laugh lines as they reminisce together about the liveliness of Gion in the 1980s when money and sake flowed with no thought of the cost of a night on the town.

Now sixty years of age and a third-generation dresser, one man learned this job from his father who had studied under his father before him. The other fellow is fifty years old. Taught by his father, he is now training a forty-year-old apprentice. Neither have plans to retire. They are busiest around 4 pm, rushing from *okiya* to *okiya* setting 15-minute records for dressing each *maiko* for her evening appointments. Spring and fall dance seasons are another extremely busy time. But during seasons when few events require their time-specific presence, they act as gofers for *geiko* who might have forgotten a cellphone at a shop or had no time to pick up a kimono from the dry cleaner's as well as escorts, especially when baggage needs to be carried. Once they get a request for help, the dressers speed off on motorbikes or bicycles, through the narrow alleys of the district, to do as bid.

Inevitably, they fend off friends and relatives who tease them about spending so much time in the company of beautiful women—something, as their boyish grins reveal, they are pleased to be reminded of.

The *otokoshi* not only dresses the *maiko*, but also escorts her on social calls.

Customers

The world of the kagai would stand on spindly legs if it were without supporters, sponsors, and clientele. For hundreds of years it was an elite class of men who revered the ideal of femininity with its implied exoticism, and who supported the world in ways that helped shape and codify modes of behavior that both sexes recognized and valued.

Regular guests may have gained access via the privilege of heredity, business acumen, politics, stage or artistic fame, but all shared an understanding of literature, traditional musical performance, and etiquette. Their access did not come easily. A new customer had to be introduced by one in good standing who would vouch that his associate had the means to afford the services available and could contribute as a guest in an affable manner.

Today, tourists may enjoy the spectacle, but without the cultural touchstones that underlie the evening, some may wonder at the expense or appeal of unintelligible songs and unrecognizable dishes. For the cultured Japanese guest, however, the evening is laden with meaning—down to the delicate morsels, served on beautiful pottery appropriate to the seasonal theme, and prepared in some of the most labor-intensive kitchens imaginable. It is a glorious treat, augmented by the women's clothing, hair ornaments, and demeanor.

Simple games are played to amuse and relax the guests, allowing them an hour or so to forget the obligations of work and family. It is a release from pressing matters, lubricated by drink and jovial company, which makes the time memorable.

Besides the cultural appeal, several men noted that the soothing voice of the women, their flattering remarks, and the gentle deferential attitudes make them feel like royalty—pampered princes—at least for an evening.

A *geiko* looks on as a *maiko* performs a *Kyomai* dance.

Two *maiko* perform a *Kyomai* dance accompanied by a *shamisen* player.

Chapter *2*

The Districts

The Five *Kagai* Districts

The Floating World, the Pleasure Quarters, the Flower-and-Willow District—all euphemisms for a realm of worldly pleasure—is woven into the fabric of Japanese nightlife.

The ancient city of Kyoto was bounded on the east by the Kamo River. Normally wide and shallow, the waterway swelled to an unruly torrent during typhoons. The unstable riverbanks were ideal for easily constructed teahouses where shopkeepers and entertainers could set up shop to serve the numerous pilgrims who visited the city's magnificent temples.

By mid-Edo Period (19th century), the city's stabilized economy fostered the rise of a merchant class. Wielding financial power and a desire for refined sensual pleasure, the merchants formed the core of the area's regular clientele, regularly frequenting *ochaya* (teahouses) where professional entertainers, *geiko* and their apprentice *maiko*, sang and danced to accompany an elegantly presented meal.

Valued for their charm and talent, the women founded various districts in which to practice their arts. In 1872, each district decided to put on dances, usually in the spring and fall. The tradition has endured for decades. In 1996, the Kyoto Traditional Musical Art Foundation, *Ookini Zaidan*, was founded to provide oversight to ensure an even distribution of work and funds to the women in these five districts. (*Ookini* means great thanks in the dialect popular in western Japan.)

During its heyday in the late 19th century, Gion was divided into Kobu (literally, top-grade part) and Higashi (east).

Snow-covered teahouses in Ponto-cho line the Kamo River (above).
The picturesque streets of Gion include a view of the Yasaka pagoda (right).

Gion Kobu

Gion Kobu, the best-known district, is on the southeast side of the Kamo River and extends to the *Ochaya*-lined street of Shinbashi, north of Shijo-dori near the willow-lined Shirakawa River. It dates back to 1665, when the Tokugawa Shogunate government granted it permission to exist. Gion's famous school of *Kyomai* dance, founded five generations ago by Yachiyo Inoue, ensures that its pupils become premier practitioners of classic Japanese dance. The district's restaurants and residences of the *geiko* and *maiko* are part of Kyoto's Preserved Historical Areas.

Miyako Odori performances are held in spring and Onshu-kai dances in autumn in Gion Kobu Theater.

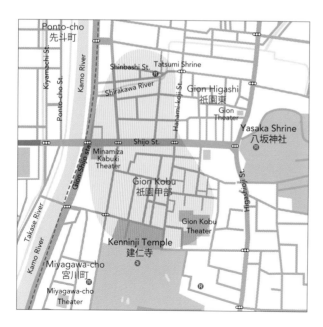

The narrow stone Tatsumi Bridge spans the Shirakawa River (above).
Traditional teahouses line Hanami-koji thoroughfare in the heart of Gion Kobu (below).

Miyako Odori spring dance revue (April 1-30) .
The Miyako Odori marked the occasion of the Kyoto Exhibition in 1872, and has been performed ever since. While men play women's roles in Kabuki, a woman dances the part of a man in this dance named "A Scene of the Cherry Blossoms of Hirano Shrine."

Onshu-kai autumn dance revue (October 1-6).
The Onshu-kai is a troupe that performs both singing and dancing. Some of the leading dancers from the Inoue School perform every autumn during the dates above. This dance is called "Butterfly Wings of Dew."

Miyagawa-cho

Miyagawa-cho is on Shijo Street, directly south of the Minamiza Kabuki Theater. After the district was designated a Historical Preserved Zone, streets where repaved and overhead wires and electrical poles reduced.

Kyo Odori performances are held in spring and Mizue-kai dances in autumn in Miyagawa-cho Theater.

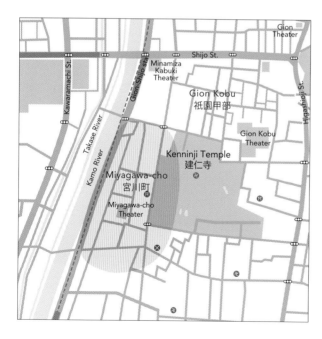

Teahouses in Miyagawa-cho (above).   Lattice frontage on a teahouse (below left).
Aglow with welcoming lanterns and curved bamboo fencing (below right).

Kyo Odori spring dance revue (first Sunday to third Sunday in April).
Starting in 1959, the *geiko* and *maiko* present especially large finales, a feature of the Wakayagi School of dance.

Mizue-kai autumn dance revue (early October).
From 2006, Miyagawa-cho restarted its fall dance tradition featuring many *geiko* and *maiko* in the dance known as "The Grand Finale of The Capital."

Ponto-cho

Ponto-cho was officially established in 1712. With many of its *ochaya* on the west side of the Kamo River, the district offers sparkling nighttime views from pavilions set over the canal that runs along the Kamo River. The watery locale cools patrons during hot summer nights. The narrow alley that runs through the district north from Shijo-dori to Sanjo-dori makes it a popular must-see for Kyoto visitors. The name, Ponto-cho, may originate from the Portuguese word for bridge, dating from a time when small slabs of stone spanned the narrow Takase River that forms the district's western edge.

    Kamogawa Odori performances are held in spring and Suimei-kai dances in autumn in Ponto-cho Theater.

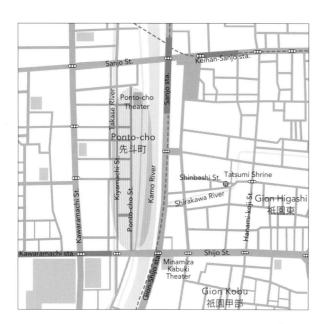

River view of the Ponto-cho Theater (above).
Ponto-cho's main thoroughfare (below).

Kamogawa Odori spring dance revue (May 1-24).
Built in 1927, the theater is a well known landmark. The dances continue through the month of May, lush with blooming wisteria, a favorite stage set.
The dance above is the "Kamogawa Odori Finale."

Suimei-kai autumn dance review (mid-October).
Performed continuously for over eighty years, the autumn dances are elegantly moving. This dance is called "Passing Autumn Showers."

Kamishichiken

Kamishichiken's history is tied to the warlord, Toyotomi Hideyoshi, who held a huge public tea ceremony in the district in 1587. More than a century before, in 1444, a fire had destroyed the Kitano Tenmangu Shrine, the heart of the area. Seven teahouses were constructed from the remains, and even today, the area's *geiko* maintain close ties with the rebuilt shrine. The women host public tea ceremonies every February when the 1,500 plum trees on the shrine grounds come into bloom. Designated a Historical Preserved Zone, the district's newly laid stone pavement and buried electrical wires enhance the beauty of the traditional architecture that lines the street leading to the east entrance of the shrine.

Kitano Odoi performances are held in spring and Kotobuki-kai in autumn in Kamishichiken Theater.

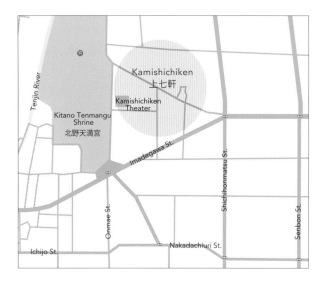

Traditional ochaya teahouses line the street in the Kamishichiken district (above).
New Year's at Kamishichiken Theater (below).

Kitano Odori spring dance revue (March 25- April 7).
The Kamishichiken district is the oldest in the *kagai*, but the dance revues started as recently as 1952.
The Hanayagi School features dances with a strong story line. The name of the dance is "Serenade."

Kotobuki-kai autumn dance revue (mid-October).
Kotobuki means happiness and this troupe presents a program very different from the spring one.
The name of the dance is "All Aboard for Good Fortune."

Gion Higashi

Gion Higashi, lies farther east, adjacent to Yasaka Shrine near the foothills of the Eastern Mountains and north of Shijo-dori between Hanami-koji and Higashi-oji. The site, formerly a samurai estate, became the home to many *ochaya*. Today, the number of teahouses has decreased, but the women of this district present their annual dance in the fall, Gion Odori, to much acclaim.

Gion Odori performances are held in autumn at Gion Theater.

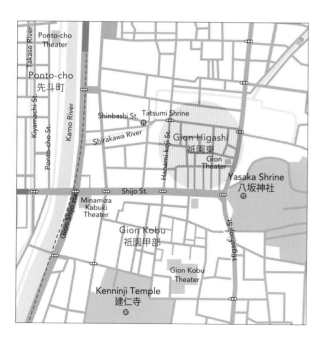

Kanki Inari Shrine has been located in the center of Gion Higasi (above).
Teahouses in this district have decreased, but several of these elegant buildings remain (below).

Yukata-kai recital (late July).
Yukata is a thin cotton *kimono* worn throught out summer. This seasonal event is a performance of *Yukata*-clad women singing *naga uta* (a long narrative song) and *kiyomoto* ballads (a lyric and narrative style song) with instrumental accompaniment, the light-colored attire and summer songs affere to eval and reflesh listenrs

Gion Odori autumn dance revue (November 1-10).
This dance revue is held only in autumn. There are fewer numbers of *geiko* and *maiko* than at other *kagai*, but their dances command appreciative audiences. This dance is "The Song of Gion Higashi", in the Fujima style of dance.

Chapter *3*

The Seasons

春 Spring

At the first glimpse of fresh green buds, Kyoto releases a collective breath, a sigh of expectation for the kaleidoscope of color and scents that season will bring. From the pale shimmering cherry blossoms to the deeper shades that form a fragile canopy of petals, spring comes in pink. A celebratory atmosphere reigns throughout; people remember that it is time to be outside, to stroll with friends, photograph a baby's first spring, and welcome new employees to share a cup of *sake* under the blossoming trees.

Nature transforms the mountains into pastel palettes, generating smiles on the most serious faces and joy at the longed-for renewal.

The colors deepen further in May as irises bloom by the thousands, and magenta-hued azalea bushes blanket the hillsides. Soon, fragrant and lush, early summer rains encourage the hydrangea to open.

Enlivening the season with spectacular dance revues, the *geiko* and *maiko* of the *kagai* districts present a festival of dance and gracious entertainment.

Tea ceremonies are performed by *maiko* and *geiko* before the spring dance revues.
Tearoom in Gion Kobu during the Miyako Odori (above) and Ponto-cho during the Kamogawa Odori (below).

桜みくじ

Maiko perform dances honoring the
gods at Heian Shrine on April 16.

The *geiko* and *maiko* of Gion Higashi pray at Kanki Inari Shrine's festival in mid May.

夏

Summer

Giant wreathes of miscanthus grass are hung from shrine *torii* gates on June 30. Kyotoites, pray that they survive the coming heat in good health by passing through these pliant reed circles. July brings the largest festival in Japan, the Gion Festival that lasts the entire month. Magnificent floats, the pride of the city, are erected, and participants are purified to be worthy to represent the local deities as the procession travels through the city streets. Men, clad in traditional wear, carry the gods, rousted from sacred homes, on a raucous ride in portable shrines through the streets.

The *geiko* and *maiko* of the *kagai* districts add grace and dignity to the procession. With low bows and offering cool refreshment, they greet the *mikoshi* shrine bearers as they pause in the Gion district for a needed rest.

In mid-summer, the spirits of the departed return for three days to rejoin the living. On the night of August 16, heads bow in farewell as ancestral spirits travel back to the nether realm, guided by the fires that burn on Kyoto's five surrounding mountains. For fifteen minutes, the city dims its lights to mark the solemn moment, and creates a collective memory.

All five *kagai* districts appear in a spectacular joint Miyako-no-Nigiwai performance the third Saturday and Sunday of June. A scene from the Nigiwai dance revue.

In early July, the *geiko* and *maiko* of Gion Kobu, along with the headmistress of the *Kyomai* dance school, Yachiyo Inoue, pray to the gods at Yasaka Shrine for better skill in dancing.

The flower-bedecked float of Gion Higashi in the *Hanagasa Junko* procession on July 24 (above).
The women of Ponto-cho perform a kabuki-style dance at Yasaka Shrine on July 24 (below).

Dressed in summer kimono, the women of all five districts fill the streets giving their greetings on *Hassaku* August 1 on the lunar callender.

Beer gardens are popular with local residents during hot summer evenings in the Kamishichiken (above) and Miyagawa-cho districts (below).

秋

Autumn

A slight dip in nighttime temperatures, sprays of minute bush clover blossoms, and the sublime fragrant olieve mark the coming of autumn. Lingering persimmons glow on the near-leafless tree limbs and scarlet red maples compete with ginko leaves aflame with golden tints. Their colors rival the rainbows that sweep across the mountains during the *shigure* rain showers that visit the city during November.

Chrysanthemums—carefully raised by amateur horticulturists—appear on household doorsteps and temple grounds. Some are tall and stately, some a cascading gush of color, and others are topped with long, spidery petals—all are the pride of their owners.

Months of dance practice culminate in the gorgeous autumn dance revues by the *geiko* and *maiko* of all five *kagai* to entertain visitors and townspeople.

Floats are paraded around the Kamishichiken district during the Zuiki (taro root) Festival on October 1-5.

Each *kagai* in turn is represented in the Jidai Festival of the Ages on October 22.

The women of Gion Kobu participate in the Kanikakuni Festival on November 8 near the Shirakawa River (above).
The *Gion Kouta* Song Festival is celebrated one *kagai* in turn on November 23 (below).

冬 Winter

The first minutes of the new year reverberate with the lingering timbre of one hundred and eight bells that are struck repeatedly beginning at midnight. Long lines of chilled shrine visitors gratefully sip a cup of warm *sake* before lighting the tip of the *okerabi*. Returning home, they twirl this twisted length of straw rope in the cold air to keep it aglow so that it can light the home hearth, ensuring the family of heat and food for the coming year.

The days lengthen until finally, tiny plum blossoms begin to scent the chill—their fragrance promising a new season, another renewal. *Geiko* and *maiko* welcome hundreds of visitors by preparing whipped powdered green tea, served with a sweet, on the grounds of Kitano Tenmangu Shrine festooned with 1,500 plum trees. And the cycle begins again.

The Kitano Tea Ceremony for the Gods is held in Kamishichiken on December 1 (above).

The women of all five *kagai* districts attend the annual Kaomise Kabuki performances in December at the Minamiza Theater (below).

The *geiko* and *maiko* of all districts pay their respects to their teachers for all their help during the year on December 13.

A Kyoto custom, a *maiko* lights the end of a twisted straw rope at midnight on December 31 to carry home and light the hearth for the new year (above).

Maiko distribute small gifts carried in the pink and white globes to extend their wishes for a prosperous year (below).

On January 7 or 9, the women of the *kagai* attend a Shinto ceremony to pray for an auspicious new year.

On January 13, the *geiko* and *maiko* of the *kagai* visit different *ochaya* to give everyone their good wishes.

All districts celebrate *Setsubun*, the division of the seasons on February 2 and 3 to banish misfortune and welcome in good luck (above).

Setsubun is also a time when the *geiko* and *maiko* attend parties dressed up in amusing costumes (below).

Every February 25, the *geiko* and *maiko* of Kamishichiken conduct tea ceremonies for the public at Kitano Tenmangu Shrine.

Preserving a Legacy

Some arts, such as Kabuki and Noh drama, are so emblematic of Japanese culture that they have been awarded the designation Intangible as World Heritages.

Many believe that the *kagai*, the flower world of *geiko* and *maiko* also approaches that standard. But despite a past association with prostitution that inhibits such a classification, the *kagai* is nonetheless a unique and respected cultural entity. The roles of *geiko* and *maiko* in preserving and continuing traditional performing arts merit extraordinary esteem, and the women's lives embody the transformative power of culture and tradition.

Entering the *kagai* is like stepping into a living museum. Although at home in the 21st century, it exhibits a code of conduct from a bygone era, and features a subculture rich in period pieces.

Indeed, the allure of the *kagai* stretches unbroken from the 17th century into our jangling modern era. And many a contemporary young Japanese girl still dreams of being elegantly clothed in gorgeous silk kimono, skilled in the performing arts, and desired at sophisticated gatherings for her charm and presence.

The future of the world of the *kagai* lies within the symbiotic nature of Japanese culture and the interconnectedness of its various aspects. The *kagai's* aesthetic side incorporates the arts of the tea ceremony, traditional music, dance and cuisine. The flower-and-willow side embodies the sensuousness of human passion and eroticism, often expressed in songs and dance based on tales of trysts and partings, unrequited passion, and the transience of life and love.

The *geiko*, who personify both the aesthetic and sensual sides, are rarified beings. But in one way, they are like women everywhere: some might have no intimate relationships and others amorous ones. The myth that they are glorified prostitutes is just that, a myth—but a potent and seductive one. For younger men, being seen in the company of a *maiko* or *geiko*, carries the provocative allure of possibility; for the elderly man, it recalls days of youthful adventures.

The very human need for these tenets of the heart to be expressed and nurtured ensures the survival of the *kagai*. The mixed pleasures of good food and wine served graciously in a beautiful setting, with amusing banter and lively conversation, bring entertaining to a higher level. A meal sprinkled with mutually understood references to an 8th century anthology of poems, 18th century songs of love and longing, and the slow measured pace of the presentation of the dishes is what clients revel in. It is an expensive pleasure and a titillating one.

Japanese culture is a collaborative effort. In a traditional tea ceremony, the host performs the ritualized movements with grace, precision, and creativity. But for the event to truly embody beauty and sophistication, the guests too, must understand and appreciate the intricate gestures and atmosphere; they must engage in the event by conversing knowledgably about the utensils, scroll, flower arrangement, and ambiance.

So too, an exquisite restaurant presenting the formal cuisine known as kaiseki, prepares its dishes to delight its customers. But fuller enjoyment comes from the diner's understanding how the meal relates to the season and is coupled with the Manyoshu, an 8th century poetry anthology. In a similar way, those who visit the teahouses frequented by *maiko* and *geiko*, share in the proper poem or song to enliven a mood and intensify a moment, bestowing conviviality on all present.

Each aspect of these shared arts joins sophisticated entertainment with knowledgeable guests to create deep cultural significance.

As one *Okiya* proprietress commented, "As long as Japanese culture exists, so will the *kagai*."

Kyoto Traditional Musical Art Foundation
—Ookini Zaidan—

The eminently elegant Spring and Autumn Dances by the *geiko* and *maiko* of Kyoto are some of the finest performances in the country. Stage settings, musicians, and dancers are showcased, and the ages-old repertoire is the delight of appreciative audiences.

The Kyoto Traditional Musical Art Foundation, established in 1996 by the Kyoto City Tourist Association and the Kyoto *Kagai* Association work together with Kyoto Prefecture, Kyoto City, Kyoto Chamber of Commerce and Industry, and related organizations to avail visitors the pleasure of seeing the best of Japan's performing arts.

These organizations collaborate to help preserve and support events that involve the arts, and to support and nurture this special heritage for future generations.

Specifically, the foundation has been responsible for the restoration of theaters in the five districts, as well as issuing grants to those studying traditional performing arts. It also offers financial support for *geiko* along with incentives to encourage their continued stage appearances.

Ookini is a typical Kyoto expression that literally means: "A big thank you".

But when the word is broken down, another interpretation reads:
O (otagai ni) each other
O (omoiyari) to think of others
Ki (kikubari shita) to be sensitive to the feelings of others
Ni (nikoyaka ni) while smiling.

Yasaka Hall, next to Gion Kobu Theater, where preformances at Gion Corner are held.

Gion Corner (http://www.kyoto-gioncorner.com/global/en.html)

Gion Corner presents a selection of seven traditional Japanese performing arts, most notably, *Kyomai* dances by *maiko*. Although not long, each performance gives the audience a taste of the rich tradition harbored in the cultural heart of Kyoto.

Popular with both Japanese and foreign visitors, Gion Corner is the only place where all types of stage performances can be seen. The *Maiko* Gallery features a video of dances. Hair ornaments and items related to the customs of the district are on display.

Kyomai dance

Bunraku puppet theatre

Gagaku court music

Kyogen theatre

Kagai Glossary

Darari-obi	freely hanging lengths of the obi sash in back
Eri	collar sewn onto an undergarment that appears at the kimono neckline
Geiko	a professional musician of traditional instruments and dancer (literally woman of the performing arts)
Juban	the robe worn under the kimono
Jikata	a woman who plays traditional instruments, usually accompanying dance
Kanzashi	hair ornaments
Maiko	an apprentice to geiko (literally dancing woman)
Kotsutsumi	small hand-held drum that rests on the shoulder and played by striking with the hand
Obi	wide sash that secures the kimono
Obiage	thin silk sash tucked into the top of the obi
Obijime	thin woven tie around the obi
Ochaya	a particular type of architecture with many small rooms in which an evening's entertainment is held, and catered food served.
Okaa-san	proprietress of the Ochaya or Okiya
Okiya	residence of the maiko and geiko
Okobo	platform-like cloven footwear of the maiko
Otokoshi	a man who dresses the women in kimono
Pocchiri	a piece of jewelry that acts as a centerpiece on the front of the obi
Shamisen	three-stringed instrument played with a plectrum
Taiko	drum placed on the floor and played with two sticks
Taiko-obi	an obi sash tucked up and rounded in back
Zashiki	an evening of entertainment with performing maiko and geiko
Zori	traditional footwear securing the foot with a thong

Bibliography

Exploring Kyoto
by Judith Clancy Stone Bridge Press
Kyoto, an Ancient Capital of Traditional Culture and Musical Art
published by Kyoto Traditional Musical Art Foundation
Little Songs of the Geisha: Traditional Japanese Ko-Uta
by Liza Dalby (Author), Liza Crihfield Dalby (Editor)
Suiko Books

Suggested viewing

Becoming a Geisha (2005) - YouTube
www.youtube.com/watch v=KrDGTUm2vBc
Mar 10, 2008 A documentary of young woman from Northern Japan who has decided move to Gion.
The Secret Life of Geisha (1999) - IMDb
www.imdb.com/title/tt0274282/combined
A documentary of the life of the Geisha. Narrated by Susan Sarandan.
The Last Geisha Madame Minako (2014)
www.youtube.com/watch v=ou57pmEDuAE
A documentary film of Madame Minako, the last geisha in Yoshiwara.
Beautiful Kyoto: Being a Maiko, featuring Fukunae-san
Discover Kyoto: Maiko or Geiko painting their faces, Kyoto 1999

Acknowledgements

Yoshio Uno, the managing director of the Ookini Zaidan proposed publishing a book about the kagai, giving me the opportunity to write about this exclusive world.

Shinichiro Kamino of Tankosha Publishing accompanied me to the interviews, smoothing out whatever awkward interpretations my inquiries might have made, and confirming the information received.

Terry J. Allan came to my aid in clarifying what I was trying to say, a difficult task when bridging language and cultural differences.

Lastly, I am grateful to the people of the kagai who made the time to answer questions, and explain their reasons for choosing to enter their professions.

Judith Clancy

Judith Clancy has lived in Kyoto since 1970. She studied
the tea ceremony at the Urasenke School of Tea and flower
arrangement with Tamura Suiko of the Ohara School of
Ikebana. Her first book, *Naturescapes*, is about Tamura's
arrangements. Other books are *Exploring Kyoto*(2006) and
Kyoto Machiya Restaurant Guide(2012), Stone Bridge Press and
Kyoto:City of Zen (2012) and *Kyoto Gardens—Masterworks of the
Japanese Gardener's Art* (2014) Tuttle. In 2012, she received the
title of Visit Kyoto Ambassador (京都国際観光大使) from the
city. She lives in a 120-year-old converted weaving studio in
Nishijin, the weaving and dyeing district of Kyoto, where she
continues to write, interpret and guide.

デザイン　　大西未生

The Alluring World of
Maiko and Geiko

平成28年1月27日　初版発行
平成28年9月28日　2版発行

著　者　Judith Clancy
編集協力　公益財団法人 京都伝統伎芸振興財団
写　真　溝縁ひろし
発行者　納屋嘉人
発行所　株式会社 淡交社
　　　　本社 〒603-8588京都市北区堀川通鞍馬口上ル
　　　　営業(075)432-5151　編集(075)432-5161
　　　　支社 〒162-0061東京都新宿区市谷柳町39-1
　　　　営業(03)5269-7941　編集(03)5269-1691
　　　　http://www.tankosha.co.jp
印刷・製本　図書印刷株式会社

©2016 Judith Clancy　溝縁ひろし　Printed in Japan
ISBN978-4-473-04059-6

落丁・乱丁本がございましたら、小社「出版営業部」宛にお送りください。送料小社負担にてお取り替えいたします。
本書のスキャン、デジタル化等の無断複写は、著作権法上での例外を除き禁じられています。また、本書を代行業者
等の第三者に依頼してスキャンやデジタル化することは、いかなる場合も著作権法違反となります。